Preparing the Liturgical Year 1:

SUNDAY AND THE PASCHAL TRIDUUM

Corbin Eddy

NOVALIS

THE LITURGICAL PRESS

Design: Eye-to-Eye Design, Toronto

Layout: Suzanne Latourelle

Illustrations: Eugene Kral

Series Editor: Bernadette Gasslein

© 1997, Novalis, Saint Paul University, Ottawa, Ontario, Canada

Business Office: Novalis, 49 Front Street East, 2nd floor, Toronto, Ontario M5E 1B3

Published in the United States of America by The Liturgical Press, Box 7500, Collegeville, MN 56321-7500

Novalis: ISBN 2 89088 799 5

The Liturgical Press: ISBN 0-8146-2487-1
A Liturgical Press Book
Library of Congress data available on request.

Excerpts from the English translations of: *The Roman Missal* © 1973, International Committee on English in the Liturgy, Inc. Used by permission. All rights reserved.

Printed in Canada.

Canadian Cataloguing in Publication Data

Eddy, Corbin, 1942-
    Preparing the liturgical year
(Preparing for liturgy)
Contents: 1. Sunday and the Paschal Triduum
    2. Lent-East and Advent-Christmas
ISBN 2089088-793-6 (v.1) -
ISBN 2-89088-890-8 (v.2)
    1. Church year. 2. Catholic Church—Liturgy.
I. Title. II. Series.
BX 1970.E33 1997   264'.02   C97-900373-3

Contents

Introduction

Life has its rhythms. The most obvious rhythm, perhaps, is nature's: spring, summer, fall and winter follow predictably upon one another, defining the activities in which we engage, and even our moods and energy levels.

Families have their own special rhythms. Birthdays, anniversaries, weekends, holidays, and religious and national feasts are observed and celebrated in various ways. It is safe to say that how families celebrate individuals, relationships, significant themes and ideals within the home is an important indicator of the overall health of the family unit.

Nations have their own distinct rhythms based on history and culture. They celebrate historical events (Bastille Day) and themes (Thanksgiving), sometimes with great patriotic fervour. Collective memory and an ability to learn from and celebrate history are important components in developing and strengthening a sense of common identity and purpose.

The Christian community, like all the world's great religious traditions, has its own rhythms. From their Jewish roots, Christians inherit a daily rhythm of prayer, a weekly rhythm with an especially sacred day, and an annual cycle of feasts and seasons called the liturgical year. Preparing a parish, or any Christian community, to celebrate the liturgical year well is not the matter of a short course or the study of a single book. It presumes a long-term, steady approach that gradually leads people to discover and experience the beauty and power of the church's liturgical traditions. This kind of approach will involve every aspect—physical, intellectual, emotional, artistic, spiritual—of the personality of individuals and of the community. It will require ongoing and steady example from the leadership of the community, carefully planned catechesis that leads people to celebrate well, and a kind of discipline and attention that distinguishes and maintains priorities.

These books are designed to help communities review their basic patterns of common worship so that these patterns may be as effective as possible in renewing the church's sense of common history, identity and mission. The sequence of the chapters is designed to help you establish some priorities. After looking at the paschal mystery, we look at the two principal celebrations of the year: Sunday and the paschal triduum. Only in light of these two feasts discussed in volume 1 do we move to reflect on the liturgical seasons of Lent-Easter and Advent-Christmas in volume 2.

Guiding Principles

1. Think prepare rather than plan. The strength of ritual-liturgical celebration lies in its stable format which links it to the prayer of the whole church. Its power arises, not from the creativity or imagination of a particular group of people, but from the whole church's experience. The participants are invited less to share in a new experience than to deepen their appreciation for and participation in a perennial expression of faith and prayer.

2. The task of preparing the liturgical year involves the ongoing education and formation of the assembly, the particular servant ministries and ordained ministers—deacon, presbyter, and bishop. The ongoing liturgical formation of a genuinely priestly people is foundational to authentic and lively celebrations.

3. Liturgy is a ritual event in the life of the church. Preparing the liturgical year requires a deep respect and reverence for the people of a particular community. You will need to consider age, language, ethnic background, as well as social and economic factors, when making choices. The rhythm of the life

of your particular community will mark the preparation. Not just the homily, but the whole of the liturgical action should connect with lived experience; the liturgical year is part of that action.

4. The lectionary and sacramentary with their pastoral notes, the *General Norms for the Liturgical Year and Calendar*, along with the liturgical calendar (*ordo*) prepared by the Canadian Conference of Catholic Bishops, provide basic resources about the seasons, reflect the tradition and present many options and much flexibility.

5. Those preparing the liturgy will need to review the many options provided in the official books so that choices make a genuine contribution to the assembly's experience of a particular celebration. They will have to keep track of the choices made from year to year, so that they can build on the foundation laid each previous year. It is neither necessary nor desirable to reinvent the way a community celebrates the seasons in our faith from year to year.

CHAPTER 1

The Paschal Mystery

The Time of Our Lives

*"Time like an ever rolling stream bears all our lives away;
They fly, forgotten as a dream dies at the opening day."*

This eighteenth-century text of Isaac Watts comprises the fifth verse of the hymn, "O God, Our Help in Ages Past." A paraphrase of Psalm 90, the hymn reflects on the meaning of time and history in light of God's eternity. It relativizes human history and contextualizes human struggles in God, who alone is "our dwelling place in all generations." Meditate on it, as both an introduction to our consideration of liturgical time and as background to a reflection on the dynamic relationship between time and eternity which the liturgical year expresses and celebrates. Individually or with members of your preparation team, look up Psalm 90 in your bible and read and reflect on it before you continue.

Time and Ritual

In ritual and celebration, believing persons and communities are brought into contact with another experience of time: certain events transcend time and link them with eternity. While God is involved with believing persons and communities at every moment of life's journey, at certain key moments we can discover God uniquely present in wonder and power. These historical moments relate in a special way to God's eternal plan for humanity and, as such, transcend history.

For Israel, these key events are its passage from slavery to freedom through the Red Sea and the blood-sealing of the covenant at Mount Sinai after it received the law that God gave to Moses. These are not ordinary events in a passing history or in the lives of people who come and go in an "ever rolling stream." The eternal significance of these events is present to and shapes all subsequent generations so that all of Israel continues to be present to these events in memory and ritual celebration. These events have perennial presence and power as they continue to define the very existence and destiny of the people of the promise. While it is true, as the prophets remind Israel, that the social and ethical consequences of the covenant are more important than the niceties of its ritual and liturgical celebration, it is hard to imagine how Israel would have survived its turbulent history without its discipline of ritual remembrance and celebration of its unique relationship with God. The wonder and energy of these events becomes present again and again as the ongoing source of Israel's identity and mission.

The Core of Christian Identity

The death and resurrection of Jesus the Christ defines the core of our Christian identity and mission. This paschal mystery is a new passover from slavery to freedom, from death to life; Christ's own blood seals a new covenant for the forgiveness of sins and calls for a new and universal reconciliation with the God whom he dares to call Abba—"Father."

In the traditional language of the liturgy, believers speak of "celebrating the sacred mysteries," or "proclaiming the mystery of faith," particularly in the eucharist which makes present Christ's saving death and resurrection, and invites us to ongoing renewal in this new covenant.

Creation

Creation is a more general kind of event that has perennial reality for both Jews and Christians and is, consequently, celebrated ritually. The creation of the universe, of the earth and of humanity cannot be understood as a once-and-for-all-event, but as an ongoing truth. In the biblical view, being and life continue to be received as gift, and humanity shares with all creation a "communion in creaturehood." This humbling sense of solidarity with the earth and the need for a gentle partnership between humanity and nature is advancing to the forefront of the religious consciousness of our time as we experience both the vastness and the relative smallness and fragility of our own planet that continues to suffer human abuse.

Catechesis

The origins of the word "catechesis" suggest the echoing and re-echoing of a truth of faith so that its content fills every aspect of a person and community's life, every period of history, and every facet of culture. In catechesis, the community proposes the death and rising of Jesus as the ultimate source of "joyful hope" for all who believe. Clearly this will involve more than traditional "book learning."

Catechesis will involve sharing personal stories, where difficulty and struggle, embraced in a right spirit, lead to new and fuller life. It will involve deeper recognition that the experience of dying and rising is common to everything that is most challenging and precious to human experience. There is dying and rising in choosing to be married, in receiving the gift of a new-born child, in the healing of a broken relationship, in dealing with a serious illness, even in experiencing the cycles of nature. The Bible is filled with events, parables, prophecies and poems which draw listeners into this central experience of life and faith. All of this comes together in Jesus' own dying and rising through which all of life is interpreted.

Art and music also express and celebrate this central way of interpreting life. As part of catechesis, they can wonderfully communicate and deepen the experience of faith. As communities pray with icons, make the stations, listen to Handel's *Messiah*, and so on, they find their experience of life deepening and expanding.

This full experience of real life in dialogue with the Bible leads persons and communities to the liturgy where God's invitation to fullness of life in Christ is continually reissued. We re-tell the central story, offer thanks and praise, and declare our

"Amen!" to the bread of life and the cup of the covenant which draw the community into the paschal mystery.

Priorities

Keeping the paschal mystery central to the life of the Christian community is the main priority in the ongoing process of liturgical renewal, and will be the priority of those responsible for preparing liturgical celebrations.

To help the community discover and articulate the experience of dying and rising as central to life, to relate that dying and rising to the Jesus story, and to celebrate that dying and rising in community are foundational priorities. What is left is for individuals and communities to develop strategies or methodologies to carry these priorities forward.

In Summary

1. The passage from death to life, the experience of renewal and rebirth is central to human experience. Every aspect of a person's life is engaged in this ongoing process of growth and change.

2. Christians see this reality lived out fully in the person of Jesus Christ and are drawn into communion with his own passage which has come to be called the paschal mystery. Believers come to full maturity as his story is told and retold within community, and as the sacraments draw them into communion with him.

3. Liturgy, which involves this word-sacrament dynamism, is celebrated from one generation to the next until fullness of life is revealed at the end of time as we know it. Preparing liturgy for people and people for liturgy is among the church's most important responsibilities.

Discussion Questions

1. Name and describe a dying and rising that took place in your life. How does your Christian faith touch this experience. How can this connection be deepened?

2. Take next Sunday's gospel passage and name or describe the kind of dying and rising to which it calls its listeners. Brainstorm possible connections between this text and the experience of your own community that catechists or homilists might use.

3. List as many examples as you can in which the Sunday liturgy expresses dying and rising. You might want to examine the penitential rite, the presentation of the gifts, the dismissal rite as some examples.

4. How can the "full, conscious, and active participation" of the faithful in the paschal mystery be deepened by our way of celebrating liturgy? Brainstorm. Dream.

CHAPTER 2

The Centrality of Sunday

Within the rhythms of a "liturgical week" and a "liturgical year," the Jewish faith focuses on the sabbath (day of rest and celebration of life as gift) and an annual cycle of feasts and seasons celebrating the great events which form Jews as a community of faith and shape their consciousness of their specific purpose, place in history, and mission.

Religious History and the Cycle of Nature

The organization of feasts and seasons blends the celebration of particular events of Jewish religious history and the cycle of nature. Nature and biblical faith interpret each other and are celebrated in a wonderful harmony. The realities of hope, promise, liberation and rebirth are celebrated at Passover, the springtime commemoration of the Exodus event. Pentecost, fifty days later, celebrates the first harvest of grain as well as the harvest of justice and righteousness lived out in the lives of all who receive the gift of the law and are sealed in the covenant of Sinai. Hanukkah, a lesser feast called the feast of lights, is another good example. Based on a miracle story involving the Maccabees family, it celebrates the rededication of the temple to God's service after its desecration by pagans. When the Maccabees came back to rededicate the temple, they found only one flask of oil to light the menorah (an eight-branch candlestick), but the small amount burned for the full eight days. This feast falls near the winter solstice, the shortest day of the year, when the sun seems to be struggling for its life and begins to return victorious.

This spirit of blending and weaving together nature and biblical history that Christians have inherited will be a very important consideration for persons involved in preparing specific celebrations.

Sunday

The celebration of Sunday is the anchor of Christian liturgy, its principle feast. Sunday celebrates creation, with all of its possibilities for dignity and order arising from God's first word, "Let there be light." Sunday celebrates Jesus' resurrection from the dead as the ultimate triumph of light over darkness, of dignity and order over disrespect and chaos. Each Sunday's celebration of the paschal mystery says "Let there be light" in a new way and at a new level.

"By a tradition handed down from the apostles and having its origin from the very day of Christ's resurrection, the church celebrates the paschal mystery every eighth day, which, with good reason, bears the name of the Lord's Day or Sunday. For on this day Christ's faithful must gather together so that, by hearing the word of God and taking part in the eucharist, they may call to mind the passion, the resurrection, and the glorification of the Lord Jesus and may thank God, who "has begotten them again unto a living hope through the resurrection of Jesus Christ from the dead" (1 Peter 1:3). Hence the Lord's Day is the first holy day of all and should be proposed to the devotion of the faithful and taught to them in such a way that it may become in fact a day of joy and of freedom from work. Other celebrations, unless they be truly of greatest importance, shall not have precedence over the Sunday, the foundation and core of the whole liturgical year" (*Constitution on the Sacred Liturgy*, #106).

Originally the Christian observance of Sunday included a counter-cultural element. The day of gathering for Christians coincided neither with the day of rest in the Greek or Roman calendars, nor with the Jewish Sabbath. The celebration of the Lord's Day stands as a constant feature of the Christian experience. As the concept of a societal day of rest coinciding with Sunday weakens in an increasingly multi-cultural and multi-religious society, it will be more important for Christian persons and communities to reclaim for themselves the specific religious, even mystical, character of the Sunday.

Ordinary Time

In the church calendar, there are about 34 Sundays in Ordinary Time. "Ordinary" comes from the word ordinal, "counted." Each Sunday's number refers to the scripture readings and prayers which the liturgical books present.

Each set of readings and prayers articulates for the community of faith an aspect of the mystery of death and resurrection which the celebration of word and sacrament uncovers. In complimentary ways, every event, prophecy, admonition, parable, and biblical image, every prayer with its use of metaphor and evocative name for God, invites participation in this mystery and calls the assembly to communion with Christ's own death and rising.

A short period of Ordinary Time falls between Christmas and Lent, while the long span of Ordinary Time, covering about half the year, falls between Easter time and Advent.

It is important to remember that Sunday retains its essential focus, even in the context of a particular season. The biblical texts for a particular season are consciously chosen to highlight certain aspects of the paschal mystery, but the paschal mystery itself remains central.

Another key to Ordinary Time is the layout of the scripture readings. The Sunday lectionary is divided into a three year cycle: Year A features Matthew's gospel, Year B, Mark's, Year C, Luke's. This arrangement flavours each year with the preoccupations of each gospel. Those preparing the liturgy need to be as familiar as possible with the unique ways in which the paschal mystery is filtered through these complimentary, yet distinctive traditions.

The semi-continuous reading of these gospels gives a sense of coherence, movement and direction to a block of Sundays. The Old Testament reading and its responsorial psalm are chosen with reference to the gospel; when we read them together carefully, we can discern a particular approach to, aspect of, or insight into the paschal mystery. This will be very helpful in planning for a particular Sunday or series of Sundays. (For more on this approach, see *Preparing the Table of the Word* in this series.)

The second reading, a semi-continuous reading of a New Testament work, has not been chosen with any specific reference to the gospel. As it adds another distinct approach to the paschal mystery, trying to harmonize it with the other readings will most often not work well.

Especially in Ordinary Time, the community's attention is often being drawn to "non-liturgical" events. The first Sunday of September, for example, falls on the Labour Day weekend which marks the beginning of a new school year. Parishes and dioceses talk of beginning a new "pastoral year." Remembrance Day and Mother's Day belong to an annual cycle of secular feasts. Themes, such as vocations, missions, right-to-life, etc. are often proposed locally or nationally for particular Sundays. Those responsible for preparing the liturgy will need to take all this into account. On the one hand, these events and themes cannot be allowed to take over the liturgy but, on the other hand, they cannot be ignored without risking separating liturgy from the concerns and observances of real life. They can often be recognized and included in the general intercessions, in the opening and/or dismissal rites, in the homily, or in the choice of a hymn. Balance, perspective, sensitivity and good taste will be essential for good judgments and decisions.

The full observance of Sunday beyond the eucharistic celebration is another important consideration. Parish events and celebrations scheduled for Sunday, special table prayers for use by families at the Sunday meal, and the celebration of evening prayer, for example, can contribute to a fuller and broader interpretation and experience of Sunday as the "Lord's Day."

The Natural Cycle

Consciousness of the natural cycle and the weather can also enrich liturgical celebration. In the northern hemisphere, for example, it seems no accident that texts concerning the passage of time, the inevitability of death, and the fragility of the earth are proclaimed in the autumn as days shorten and nights lengthen. The weather itself becomes a part of the liturgical environment. The careful use of colour (darker shades of green, the colour of Ordinary Time), dried plant and flower arrangements at the entrance to the church, or a mellower approach to music can all help focus the assembly's attention on the particular flavour of the paschal mystery on a particular Sunday or block of Sundays.

Catechesis

Catechesis on the centrality of Sunday will need to be ongoing to plumb the depths of the experience into which Sunday invites believers. The content of this basic catechesis might be summarized as follows: Genesis 1 describes God's creation of the universe in six days. On the seventh day, the Sabbath, God rested. Sunday, the first day of the week is also called the Eighth Day—a day that transcends "earthly time," and "earthly Sabbath." It heralds a new creation. Sunday is about renewal and recreation in light of the eternal destiny to which we are called. It is the Lord's Day.

On Sundays, the community gathers for eucharist, a joyful banquet with the risen Lord and a sacrifice of praise and thanksgiving which prefigures the eternal feast of heaven. On this day, God began the work of creation by saying "Let there be light." On this day Jesus rose victorious over the darkness of sin and death. On this day the Spirit came in wind and fire. On this day the community of believers continues to be bathed in this light, especially conscious of its identity and call to herald this good news to the whole world.

The lectionary will also be an important source of ongoing catechesis on the meaning and centrality of the paschal mystery to Sunday. Read and pray over the texts, discerning and appropriating the aspects or facets of the paschal mystery which emerge from them and give each Sunday its own texture.

In Summary

1. Sunday, the day itself, and the eucharist which finds its most natural home there, celebrate the core mystery of the Christian faith. "Christ has died; Christ is risen; Christ will come again."

2. In rest and freedom, in word and sacrament, in joy and hope, Christian communities are nourished and renewed in the context and consequences of the paschal mystery.

Discussion Questions

1. Describe a typical Sunday in your own life. How could this be enhanced in light of Christian tradition?

2. How does our community prepare the Sunday liturgy? How might this preparation process be enhanced or expanded?

3. How might our community and our families recapture the uniqueness of Sunday in an increasingly multi-cultural or secular society?

4. Are the assembly, the table of the word, and the table of the eucharist truly central in our experience of Sunday eucharist? How could we deepen our appreciation of these basics?

5. Review all the ministries that currently serve the Sunday assembly. How are persons prepared for these ministries? How is the effectiveness of these ministries encouraged and evaluated?

6. Could our community do anything more to celebrate Sunday—for example, social gatherings, evening prayer?

CHAPTER 3

The Paschal Triduum

As the central feast in the rhythm of the church's liturgy is Sunday, so the central Sunday in the annual rhythm of feasts and seasons is Easter. It used to be said in popular catechesis that every Sunday is a "little Easter." Upon further reflection, it is probably better to say that Easter is a "big Sunday." It is such a big Sunday that it has a forty-day preparatory period and overflows into a fifty-day celebration.

What Is a Triduum?

The first thing to recognize about the paschal triduum from which the Easter season flows is that it is celebrated as a triduum—one unified celebration lasting three days—which, with special intensity, leads believers into the paschal mystery and forms the centre and heart of the liturgical year. The three days of the triduum are calculated as follows: Day 1—Thursday evening to Friday evening; Day 2—Friday evening to Saturday evening; Day 3—Saturday evening to Sunday evening. We need to see and celebrate the triduum, not as the last three days of Lent or as three separate events in the life of Christ, but as a single feast.

The entrance antiphon for the Mass of the Lord's Supper, which begins the triduum, emphasizes the overarching principle of unity: "We should glory in the cross of our Lord Jesus Christ, for he is our salvation, our life and our resurrection; through him we are saved and made free" (Galatians 6:4). This wonderful text invites us, not simply to recall Christ's death and resurrection, but to enter into it in a specific way. To do this, we need to overcome the tendency to approach liturgy as historical drama. Christians do not pretend to be at the last supper, at the foot of the cross, or in the garden of the resurrection;

rather we recognize ourselves as actively participating and living out the mystery of Christ's death and resurrection *today*.

In preparing the great liturgical celebration of the triduum, it will be important to seek ways of expressing the unity of the whole, while at the same time respecting and expressing the unique dignity and power of each component part.

The principle focus of the triduum is the celebration of initiation at the Easter vigil with those who, for the first time, enter the tomb with Christ and rise with him in the sacraments of baptism, confirmation and eucharist.

An important clue to the unity of the three days is the single entrance antiphon at the Mass of the Lord's Supper and the single solemn dismissal at the end of the Easter vigil. There are no entrance songs or dismissals at intermediate stages. The whole celebration unfolds and takes up each day from where it left off. In preparing the triduum, you will need to emphasize this unity in ways that invite the assembly to participate in the whole feast. Appointing the same presider and homilist for each of the principal rites is one effective means of drawing the celebration together.

Although strictly speaking not theatre, the liturgy has elements of drama and choreography which will communicate well only if well-performed. Especially during the triduum, the quality of proclamation, song, gesture and presidential style needs to reflect the community's best efforts. Gestures such as the foot-washing, prostration, bringing in and venerating the cross, carrying the paschal candle and distributing light at the vigil, and sharing in holy communion in the blessed bread and cup need careful attention to detail, perhaps even rehearsal.

Making the Triduum Truly Central

Preparing the triduum involves more than preparing the specific rites, as important as these preparations are. It will involve preparing the whole parish community to understand and embrace the triduum as truly central to its life of faith, the most important coming together of the entire year. Parish leadership will want to work at building a spirit and tradition around the triduum, for example, developing the expectation that, as the core of the parish, all involved in parish council, liturgical ministries, service ministries etc. will want to participate; that all music ministries will combine their resources for these celebrations; that those preparing for the sacraments of initiation be well integrated into the community, especially as the triduum draws near, so that all will want to be at the vigil to support them. Mere exhortation to come is never enough.

The major rituals, as outlined in the official books, provide a very rich invitation to experience and celebrate beautiful worship. Because they are so central and are celebrated once a year, they will require very little innovation. Planners will concentrate on care and reverence so that this annual event in the life of the community will be comfortable, yet powerful. Annual rituals such as these find their strength in their substantial sameness. Rather than planning innovations, take care to deepen the ritual experience while maintaining its classic shape. Especially in the triduum, fully using the basic prescribed symbols and actions speaks more eloquently than adding secondary or merely decorative elements.

Day 1: Thursday Evening – Friday Evening

The Mass of the Lord's Supper

The opening rites of the Mass of the Lord's Supper include singing the Glory to God and ringing bells. Omitted during the forty days of Lent, these two actions actually indicate that Lent is over! After the Glory to God, the liturgy becomes rather more subdued, as we enter a different period of even more intense prayer and fasting. All the readings direct the community's attention to the paschal mystery with images such as the blood of the lamb on a doorpost, the breaking of bread and the washing of feet.

The washing of feet is a kind of visual homily. This symbol of the foundation of Christian life should be expressed as fully as possible. It will be most effective if the assembly can clearly see, feel and participate in the action. As participants move to their places, large basins and towels will be carried forward, accompanied by singing. Note that the sacramentary does not mandate any number of participants. The washing of the feet, like eucharist itself, is more than historical re-enactment. The living Christ is made present as "you wash one another's feet." Consider setting up stations in various parts of the church: seniors, children, persons with special needs could be included as a sign of the community's commitment to service in Jesus' name. Other parish leaders could join the presider in washing the feet of fellow parishioners.

As part of the preparation of table and gifts, the ritual invites the community to present gifts for the poor along with bread and wine. The collection at this liturgy must not be perceived as "just another collection," but can embody and conclude the community's Lenten almsgiving efforts.

Rich and full symbols should mark this eucharistic celebration. Offer communion from the cup; use bread or hosts large enough to be broken for the people. Break sufficient bread or hosts to accommodate the large gathering anticipated on Good Friday; although this takes a bit more time, eucharistic ministers can share in this powerful sign of communion in one body broken and given. The litany, with its repetitive "Lamb of God," sung until the action is completed, can be particularly touching on Holy Thursday. Likewise it is especially appropriate that eucharistic ministers gather at the table after the assembly's communion and prepare to take communion immediately from this liturgy to the housebound.

The concluding procession bearing the eucharist (preferably to a separate chapel) has very ancient roots. It reminds the community that in former times the eucharist was reserved, not in the principle gathering place of the assembly, but in another location specifically designed for this purpose and having its own character and dignity. This practice is still recommended today. Invite members of the community to keep vigil in this chapel until midnight. If the liturgy of hours forms an integral part of the triduum, you could celebrate night prayer at midnight.

The Celebration of the Lord's Passion

The principal liturgy of Good Friday, and the second of Day 1 of the triduum, is the Celebration of the Lord's Passion, ordinarily scheduled for 3:00 in the afternoon. Parishes accustomed to daily morning eucharist may wish to schedule morning prayer from the liturgy of hours at the normal mass time on Good Friday and Holy Saturday. Where Good Friday is not a holiday, consider having the Celebration of the Lord's Passion in the early evening to allow for full participation.

A silent assembly and bare environment set the tone for this celebration. It begins with a simple entrance of the presider: the ministers prostrate themselves as the assembly kneels for silent prayer. The opening prayer follows. It is striking that the traditional sign of the cross and greeting are omitted, a signal that this is the continuation of one great liturgy which began the evening before. The act of prostration and kneeling, humbling signs of emptiness before the great mystery, as well as sorrow for sin, are important gestures which must be and feel significant.

Take care to see that the very best readers proclaim the powerful texts appointed for this day. Give special attention to the passion. Discourage the assembly's participation in the crowd parts while the rest of the text is divided among a narrator and principal figures in the account. Consider a number of positive possibilities: the chanting of the text by three able singers, the proclamation of the text by one or several lectors, in which each takes a section while the assembly sings acclamations.

The solemn intercessions of the day can be a powerful sign of the church's ongoing commitment to the whole world in a ministry of prayer. The second reading offers a wonderful invitation to be in communion with Jesus whose suffering and prayer are one reality.

> *Let us approach the throne of grace with boldness, so that we may receive mercy and find grace to help in time of need. In the days of his flesh, Jesus offered up prayers and supplications, with loud cries and tears, to the one who was able to save him from death, and he was heard because of his reverent submission (Hebrews 4).*

Explore and then rehearse with those who will lead these prayers the possibilities for kneeling, for more extended silences and sung acclamations so that these intercessions may be experienced as a smoothly unified whole.

The veneration of the cross can be a wonderful and dramatic gesture by the whole assembly. Encourage a processional format which involves the whole assembly. The community may choose to use its regular processional cross or a larger wooden cross which would have more visual prominence. Bringing the cross into the worship area with the three stops and accompanying acclamation is the preferred option, especially since it matches the carrying in of the paschal candle with its three stops and acclamations at the Easter vigil. When rehearsing these two gestures, be sure to indicate that the ministers carrying the cross and the candle should stop at the same three places. To highlight and amplify the role of these symbols at the heart of the liturgical year gives them a renewed perspective and sets them in their place of honour.

After the veneration of the cross, the eucharist is transferred from a side chapel and the assembly comes forward in procession once more, this time for communion. The remaining eucharist, to be used only in ministry to the dying on Holy Saturday, is carried to an appropriate place outside the main worship area. The presider offers a prayer over the people and the liturgy concludes in silence; once more there is no dismissal rite.

Day 2: Friday Evening – Saturday Evening

The most distinctive characteristic of the second day of the triduum is its lack of a principal liturgical celebration.

A simple night prayer in the tradition of the liturgy of hours would be very appropriate on Good Friday evening, but no elaborate celebration, such as a dramatic portrayal of the stations of the cross or passion play, which would obscure or compete with the principal liturgy of the day, is appropriate. A new liturgical day has begun; such devotions would take the community back to the focus of Day 1.

While you can celebrate morning prayer and the preparatory rites with the elect on Holy Saturday morning and afternoon, an "empty-feeling" day of anticipation seems the best approach. An important focus for entering into the spirit of this time of "empty anticipation" is the tradition of the paschal fast. "Let the paschal fast be kept sacred. Let it be observed everywhere on Good Friday and, where possible, prolonged through Holy Saturday, as a way of coming to the joys of the Sunday of the resurrection with uplifted and welcoming heart" (*Constitution on the Sacred Liturgy*, 110).

The paschal fast is distinct from the Lenten fast. It is not penitential, but anticipatory. It is an emptying so to better appreciate the feast, a time of silence so that the festive music might be more exciting. The fast and the silence focus our attention on the great festival ahead.

While only strictly prescribed for Good Friday, the spirit of the fast calls for extension into Holy Saturday (*Rite of Christian Initiation of Adults*, 172). It is important that communities find ways to observe a common fast and a common silence in solidarity with those preparing for baptism or reception into full communion at the Vigil.

Day 3: Saturday Evening – Sunday Evening

The Vigil at Night

The Easter Vigil takes place at night. This time frame is a non-negotiable item. A *Circular Letter Concerning the Preparation and Celebration of the Easter Feasts* (Prot. N. 126:88) from the Congregation for Divine Worship expresses this imperative in the strongest possible language. "The entire celebration of the Easter Vigil takes place at night. It should not begin before nightfall; it should end before daybreak on Sunday. This rule is to be taken according to its strictest sense. Reprehensible are those abuses and practices which have crept in many places in violation of this ruling, whereby the Easter Vigil is celebrated at the time of day that it is customary to celebrate anticipated Sunday masses" (78).

Reasons for ignoring this rubric, such as lack of public order, are not put forward in connection with Christmas night or other gatherings. The power and energy of the light of Christ cannot be adequately expressed or experienced apart from an experience of darkness. The fire is precisely that: a real bonfire around which people gather. Fires such as this have a primitive universal appeal. The fire, which is our safety, security and place of gathering, is a tangible sign of who God is for us. From this primitive fire the light of Christ dawns upon the world.

Lighting the paschal fire and reading the creation account in the light of the paschal candle can have profound implications and can strengthen awareness and celebration of the unity of all creation. The renewal of the earth and the regeneration of life which springtime brings are celebrated even in the secular signs of the season—eggs, flowers, rabbits, new clothes. In families and communities, these elements and feelings are incorporated into the mystery of Christ whose resurrection brings newness of life to all human experience.

You will need to detail carefully the preparation and lighting of the paschal candle and the procession which follows. How will the light be spread throughout the church? How will the ushers and ministers of hospitality serve the gathering of the assembly? These details are very important, as is a brief but significant silence in candlelight before the cantor or deacon sings the Exsultet. If you don't turn on the electric lights until after this proclamation of the resurrection is completed, the light, and even the smell, of the burning candles can have their full impact.

The readings of the vigil proclaim the whole sweep of biblical hope and promise which explode in the resurrection of Jesus. For this reason, do not deprive your community of this panorama of salvation. Those who gather for the vigil expect a full celebration. Efforts to abbreviate or truncate the celebration by eliminating texts and taking short cuts with the ritual gestures do a disservice.

You will also need to prepare well the singing of the alleluia which was "buried" during Lent, as well as the gospel procession which it accompanies. A procession around the assembly with gospel book held high, accompanied by candles, incense, and even banners can highlight the glory of the Easter message the gospel reveals.

The homily will need careful preparation. At best it will pull together the great images of the biblical texts, creating a bridge to the sacraments of initiation that follow. Creation, passage to freedom, invitation to the feast still happen among us. We continue to live the story.

After the homily, the sacraments of initiation unfold. To minimize confusion and distraction you will need to be sensitive to the numbers of catechumens and candidates for full communion, as well as the physical layout of the building. Because there is so much to see, hear, even smell, choose acclamations that the assembly can sing almost spontaneously during the celebration of initiation so that books or other participation aids are unnecessary. The litany of saints, which invites into the action our Christian ancestors from every age, is a particularly powerful accompaniment to the procession to the baptistry. Including sung acclamations with the blessing of the font can also be an effective way of helping the assembly give thanks for the waters of life and renewal.

Rich and full symbols should mark the eucharistic table at this celebration, too. The breaking of bread and pouring of wine in which the living presence of the risen Christ is shared, and the reception of persons at the table for the first time is likewise crucial to a full experience of the vigil.

Continue to welcome newcomers and celebrate community in Christ with a social gathering afterwards.

Easter Sunday

The eucharist of Easter Day basks in the light of the vigil. A challenge for those preparing the celebration is the presence of many participants who are not usually members of the assembly. This challenges regular parishioners and ministers to both be and speak the Easter message of peace and victory over sin and alienation. Plan to sing traditional Easter hymns that as many as possible will know; bring forward into the morning celebrations some elements of the vigil by highlighting the alleluia and gospel procession as well as the renewal of baptismal promises and sprinkling rite.

Closing the triduum late on Easter Sunday evening with paschal vespers or evening prayer may seem more than a community can realistically celebrate. Still it bears serious consideration. A core of parishioners who have participated fully during Lent and throughout the triduum may well appreciate this opportunity. The core can grow larger every year. Even a small group gathered in the baptistry can offer this prayer together in the name of the whole church.

Catechesis

Forming a community to fittingly celebrate the triduum is cumulative. It will rely heavily on how Christian initiation is integrated into the community. It will be rooted in how Lenten preaching and celebration lead into it, and Easter preaching and celebration flow out of it from year to year. Everything a community does should form it to celebrate the triduum.

A more direct, intentional catechesis would work as follows. Parish groups or organizations (pastoral council, prayer group, Knights of Columbus, etc.) that meet during Lent would spend the bulk of their meetings learning about and reflecting on the triduum. The same organizations would take a similar approach to meetings during Easter, perhaps including R.C.I.A. team members, newly baptized or confirmed persons, etc. Consciously naming the triduum and the initiation sacraments as parish priorities can complement the more general community focus during Lent and Easter.

Priorities

Priorities for planning the triduum will focus on encouraging and facilitating the "full, conscious and active participation" of all in the celebration, stressing and reinforcing in whatever way possible the unity of the triduum, the centrality of the initiation sacraments to the ongoing life of the church, and the need to bring together in a collaborative way all the ministries of the community so that the celebration is an expression of the community at its fullest and best.

Discussion Questions

1. Is the triduum truly central to the life of our parish? How do we know?

2. What would we need to do to enhance its centrality?

3. When we think "triduum," do we think one celebration or three? How can we highlight the unity of the triduum? You might want to consider music, ministers, environment.

4. What are the connections between your parish liturgical celebrations throughout the year and the triduum? How can your parish liturgical practices through the year enhance your celebration of the triduum? How does your celebration of the triduum influence your celebrations throughout the year?

In Summary

The chart below reviews the triduum as a whole, visualizes its basic flow so you can identify the paschal mystery embodied there, and prepare accordingly.

Day	Liturgical Celebration	Gesture	Focus: paschal mystery
1	Mass of the Lord's Supper	footwashing collection for the poor; breaking of bread, sharing of cup of life	self-emptying; service
	Night Prayer		
	Morning Prayer		
	Celebration of the Passion	prostration; proclamation of the passion; veneration of the cross	cross of glory
2	Night Prayer	Paschal fast	silence of tomb
	Morning Prayer		
	Rites of RCIA for Holy Saturday		preparation
3	Vigil of Easter	Fire, story, water, renewal of baptismal promises; bread and wine	light conquering darkness; story of stories; new birth; covenant meal
	Easter Day	water, story, new birth, renewal of baptismal promises, bread and wine	covenant meal
	Evening prayer	fire, water, praise.	rejoicing at God's wonders

Glory Days

"Christ redeemed us all and gave perfect glory to God particularly through his paschal mystery: dying he destroyed our death and rising he restored our life. Therefore the Easter triduum of the passion and resurrection of Christ is the culmination of the entire liturgical year. Thus the solemnity of Easter has the same kind of preeminence in the liturgical year that Sunday has in the week.

"The Easter triduum begins with the evening Mass of the Lord's Supper, reaches its high point in the Easter Vigil, and closes with evening prayer on Easter Sunday." (General Norms for the Liturgical Year and Calendar [GNLYC], 18-19)

"We should glory in the cross of our Lord Jesus Christ for he is our salvation, life and resurrection; through him we are saved and set free." Entrance antiphon, Mass of the Lord's Supper

Glorying in the Cross

The title of the chart, "Glory Days," at the end of this book, highlights one of the most fundamental characteristics of this feast that lasts for three days: it is not a chronological celebration of several events in the Lord's life, but a single feast that, in each day's readings, gestures and symbols, catches the different hues of the glory of the paschal mystery. Of this glory, Bishop Raymond Lahey has written: "To celebrate the day of the Lord's death is to glory in the cross, to draw nourishment from the banquet that unites us to it, and to commit ourselves to the loving service that the cross demands, so to enter the risen life it brings" ("Re-thinking the Easter Triduum, Part 1," *Celebrate!*, January-February 1996, 16-18).

Keeping track of all these readings, gestures and symbols can be challenging for those preparing these liturgies and, literally, seeing these celebrations as part of a whole is often impossible if we can only flip pages in a book. This chart is designed to help planners see the triduum "at a glance." The chart highlights six aspects of liturgical preparation.

Who's Doing What?

The first column looks at who's doing what? The assembly figures large in this presentation: we never designate only a lector or presbyter the minister of a celebration, since the assembly's role never disappears. Everything possible must be done, therefore, to promote its "full, conscious and active participation demanded by the liturgy." (For more on this topic, see *Preparing and Evaluating Liturgy* in this series.)

Music

The second column deals with music. There is a lot of music in the triduum; a frequent error is thinking that it all has to be different. Another error is forgetting that much of it is meant to accompany *processions*. When selecting music for the triduum, keep the following questions in mind: What is the ritual action? What is the size of the space in which this action will take place? What music best matches these two? What does the assembly know?

Basics

The third column, named "Basics," reminds you of the things you mustn't forget. Do you have towels for the washing of feet? Have you appointed people to hold the cross while the people venerate it? Do you have white garments for the baptized? Did you buy incense? Did someone get the tapers? Sometimes these are the most overlooked of all the things we are preparing!

Intensifying the Ritual

The fourth column, borrowing an image from master chefs who regulate the heat for their creations carefully, identifies how you can "turn up the ritual heat." Those preparing liturgy can make conscious decisions about how engaging the ritual will be. Generous use of symbol, ample gestures in which the whole assembly can participate, to give just two examples, draw people into the liturgy more deeply. Attention to detail here can engage people more deeply; lack of such attention can leave them uninvolved.

Connections with the Rest of the Year

The fifth column links this celebration with other liturgies we celebrate during the year. If planners think that the triduum stands totally apart from the rest of our celebrations, the amount of work to be done seems overwhelming. But when we see that this is not just a once-a-year event, we can discover how the energy invested in preparing these celebrations can pay dividends all through the year.

Special Skills

The last column features the special skills that the triduum demands. Remember, however: these are never used only once.

Bernadette Gasslein

Bernadette Gasslein, senior editor at Novalis, is editor of the Preparing for Liturgy *series, and author of* Preparing and Evaluating Liturgy. *She originally prepared this chart as a teaching tool.*

Moveable Feasts, 1998-2030

Year	Ash Wednesday	Easter	Pentecost
1998	Feb 25	Apr 12	May 31
1999	Feb 17	Apr 4	May 23
2000	Mar 8	Apr 23	June 11
2001	Feb 28	Apr 15	June 3
2002	Feb 13	Mar 31	May 19
2003	Mar 5	Apr 20	June 8
2004	Feb 25	Apr 11	May 30
2005	Feb 9	Mar 27	May 15
2006	Mar 1	Apr 16	June 4
2007	Feb 21	Apr 8	May 27
2008	Feb 6	Mar 23	May 11
2009	Feb 25	Apr 12	May 31
2010	Feb 17	Apr 4	May 23
2011	Mar 9	Apr 24	June 12
2012	Feb 22	Apr 8	May 27
2013	Feb 13	Mar 31	May 19
2014	Mar 5	Apr 20	June 8
2015	Feb 18	Apr 5	May 24
2016	Feb 10	Mar 27	May 15
2017	Mar 1	Apr 16	June 4
2018	Feb 14	Apr 1	May 20
2019	Mar 6	Apr 21	June 9
2020	Feb 26	Apr 12	May 31
2021	Feb 17	Apr 4	May 23
2022	Mar 2	Apr 17	June 5
2023	Feb 22	Apr 9	May 28
2024	Feb 14	Mar 31	May 19
2025	Mar 5	Apr 20	June 8
2026	Feb 18	Apr 5	May 24
2027	Feb 10	Mar 28	May 16
2028	Mar 1	Apr 16	June 4
2029	Feb 14	Apr 1	May 20
2030	Mar 6	Apr 21	June 9

GLOSSARY

Baptismal renewal: A repetition by the Christian community of vows made initially at baptism to reject sin and evil and to profess faith in God (Father, Son, and Holy Spirit) in union with the church. Takes place whenever the sacraments of baptism or confirmation are celebrated to affirm solidarity in faith and mission with newly baptized-confirmed. Takes place in an especially solemn way at Easter.

Baptistry: Separate building or designated part of the church where baptism is celebrated.

Blood sealing: In the covenant ritual (Ex 24), the blood of the lamb is dashed upon the altar, representing God, and on the people, signifying that these covenant partners hare a common life. The lamb is subsequently consumed by the people and by the altar's fire as a further sign of communion. The blood of the eucharist in the New Testament is a departure from Hebrew ideas in that the blood is proposed as drink, but the significance of blood as life communicated from Jesus (the lamb of God) to his disciples through the eucharistic feast is, in fact, intensified.

Candidates for full communion: Persons already baptized in a Christian church and participating in further formation prior to reception into the Roman Catholic Church through confirmation and eucharist.

Covenant: A pact between two parties to be faithful to each other according to set agreements. In the Bible, the term refers primarily to the solemn relationship entered into by God with the people of Israel (Ex 24). God promises to be faithful to Israel while inviting Israel's corresponding fidelity in keeping the Law. Sealed and renewed in ritual (cf Blood sealing above).

End Time: Refers to the culmination and completion of life as we know it. The ultimate destiny of all persons of all humanity, and of all creation. Begun and heralded in the death and resurrection of Christ who leads all humanity and all the world into a new creation to be fully revealed at the end of time.

Evening Prayer: A traditional form of Christian prayer, drawn largely from the Bible and celebrated by the community toward the end of day. Often called Vespers.

Gospel Procession: The solemn carrying of the Book of the Gospels to the place from which the gospel of the day will be proclaimed. Accompanied (except during Lent) by the singing of Alleluia.

Lectionary: A book containing texts from the Bible arranged for use in liturgical services.

Mystagogy: The continuing introduction of newly baptized persons into the full, ongoing meaning and consequences of the way of life into which they have been initiated through the sacraments. It involves the incorporation and integration of new members into the fullness of the community's life of worship and service through prayer, teaching, and the experience of the Christian life.

Priestly people: Derives from the ancient concept of priest as one who offers sacrifice to God in the name of a people—a kind of mediator between that people and God. Pre-Christian ideas of priesthood are raised to a new level in Christ, as his sacrifice of himself reconciles all humanity to God one and for all. Especially in the sacraments of initiation (baptism, confirmation, eucharist), believers are drawn into communion with his sacrifice and are called to be "through him, with him, and in him" a living sacrifice of praise and thanksgiving for the peace and reconciliation made possible through his death and resurrection.

Ritual: The established order of words and gestures prescribed for a public ceremony, usually religious or civic.

Sacramentary: A book containing prayers and directions for the presiding bishop or presbyter (priest) at the eucharist and rites connected with it.

Scrutinies: Literally a testing of persons preparing for baptism. A ritual involving an expression on their part of willingness to live the challenging call of the gospel, and prayers (exorcisms) for the healing of all in them that is weak, defective, or sinful and for the strengthening of all that is upright, strong, and good.

Solstice: Either of the two times of the year when the sun is at its greatest distance from the celestial equator; about June 21, when the sun reaches its northernmost point on the celestial sphere or about December 22 when it reaches its southernmost point. The winter solstice, for example, in the northern hemisphere (December 22) marks the longest night of the year and heralds the beginning of the gradual lengthening of days. Significant in the establishment of seasons and religious feasts related to the cycles of nature.

Recommended Reading

Books

Adam, Adolph. *The Liturgical Year: Its History and Meaning After the Reform of the Liturgy*, (N.Y.: Pueblo, 1981). A classic.

Bonneau, Normand, O.M.I. *The Sunday Lectionary: Ritual Word, Paschal Shape*, (Collegeville: Liturgical Press, 1998).

Days of the Lord (seven vols.) (Collegeville: Liturgical Press, 1990-1994). Owners will reach for it every week.

Mick, Lawrence E. *Sourcebook for Sundays and Seasons*, (Chicago: LTP, published annually). Something for every day of the church year.

Nocent, Adrian, O.S.B. *The Liturgical Year*, (Collegeville: Liturgical Press, 1977). Published in six volumes.

Talley, Thomas *The Origins of the Liturgical Year* (N.Y.: Pueblo, 1986). A classic, but hard reading for the uninitiated.

Whalen, Michael D. *Seasons and Feasts of the Church Year* (Mahwah, N.J.: Paulist Press, 1992). An excellent popular introduction.

Periodicals

Celebrate! Novalis, 49 Front Street, 2nd floor, Toronto, Ontario, Canada M5E 1B3. Award-winning Canadian liturgical periodical; topical articles; commentaries for Sundays and feasts.

liturgical ministry. Liturgical Press, Saint John's Abbey, Collegeville, Minnesota 56321-7500. Scholarly and pastoral focuses characterize this journal.

National Bulletin on Liturgy. Publications Service, Canadian Conference of Catholic Bishops, 90 Parent Avenue, Ottawa, Ontario, Canada K1N 7B1

Today's Liturgy, Oregon Catholic Press, 5536 NE Hassalo, Portland, Oregon 97213-3638. Focuses on music ministers.